TRANSPORTATION

Joanne Mattern

BLACKBIRCH® PRESS

© 2004 by Blackbirch Press. Blackbirch Press is an imprint of Thomson Gale, a part of the Thomson Corporation.

Thomson is a trademark and Gale [and Blackbirch Press] are registered trademarks used herein under license.

For more information, contact
The Gale Group, Inc.
27500 Drake Rd.
Farmington Hills, MI 48331-3535
Or you can visit our Internet site at http://www.gale.com

ALL RIGHTS RESERVED
No part of this work covered by the copyright hereon may be reproduced or used in any form or by any means—graphic, electronic, or mechanical, including photocopying, recording, taping, Web distribution or information storage retrieval systems—without the written permission of the publisher.

Every effort has been made to trace the owners of copyrighted material.

Picture Credits

Cover: Library of Congress (top), NASA (bottom)
AP/Wide World Photos, 28 (bottom)
© Art Today, Inc., 8, 14, 21, 24
© Bettmann/CORBIS, 5, 7 (bottom), 16 (top), 18 (bottom), 22, 23
© British Museum, 4 (bottom)
© COREL Corporation, 27, 30
© Historical Picture Archive/CORBIS, 6 (bottom)
© Hulton-Deutsch Collection/CORBIS, 16 (bottom)
© Lake County Museum/CORBIS, 19
Library of Congress, 15, 17, 18 (top), 20, 22 (insets, both)
© Mary Evans Picture Library, 4 (top), 7 (top), 10, 11 (bottom), 13 (both)
NASA, 28 (top), 29 (both)
© North Wind Picture Archives, 6 (top), 9 (all), 11 (top), 12
© Mark Peterson/CORBIS, 31
© Underwood & Underwood/CORBIS, 25
© USAF Museum Photo Archives, 26

LIBRARY OF CONGRESS CATALOGING-IN-PUBLICATION DATA

Mattern, Joanne, 1963–
    Transportation / by Joanne Mattern.
        p. cm. — (Yesterday and today)
    Includes bibliographical references and index.
    ISBN 1-56711-835-6 (hardback : alk. paper)
    1. Transportation—Juvenile Literature. [1. Transportation.] I. Title. II. Series.

TA1149.M35 2004
388—dc22
                                                                    2004008389

Printed in the United States
10 9 8 7 6 5 4 3 2 1

Table of Contents

On the Move   4

On the Water   6

Exploring the World   8

Carriages and Wagons   10

Sails and Steam   12

The Age of Steam   14

The First Automobiles   16

Automobiles and Motorcycles Take over the Roads   18

Trucks and Highways   20

Taking to the Air   22

Changing Trains   24

Flying Fast   26

Space Travel   28

Transportation Today   30

Glossary   32

For More Information   32

Index   32

On the Move

People have always needed to get from one place to another. Today there are all sorts of ways to travel, but things were very different six thousand years ago.

Before about 3500 B.C., people had to use their own power to move from place to place. The simplest way to travel was on foot, but walking was slow and tiring.

People also used animals to travel. Animals such as horses, camels, donkeys, oxen, and elephants carried people and their goods from place to place. Animals such as dogs, reindeer, and horses were also used to pull sleds.

About 3500 B.C., the wheel was invented. The earliest

When the wheel was invented about 3500 B.C., people developed wagons and carts (below) and were no longer limited to using animals alone (above) for transportation.

wheels were made in Mesopotamia, in the Middle East. The first wheels were made of stone. They were solid and did not have spokes. Spoked wheels appeared around 2700 B.C. Spokes made the wheel lighter and easier to use.

The wheel was one of the most important inventions of all time. Without the wheel, most forms of land transportation would not be possible. The wheel led to the invention of carts and wagons, which could be pulled by humans or animals. This allowed heavier loads to be carried easily and quickly.

People also rode in carts. The ancient Romans rode in wheeled carts called chariots. Chariot races were a popular form of entertainment.

Chariot Races

Chariot racing was a popular sport in ancient Rome. Spectators packed an arena called the Circus Maximus and cheered for their favorite teams. Many spectators also placed bets on which teams would win.

Chariots usually had a team of four horses controlled by one driver. Ten to twenty races were held on a typical day, with four to twelve teams competing in each race. Chariot drivers could be freemen or slaves who had been specially trained. Successful drivers could win a lot of money and have their names engraved on stone monuments. If a slave won, his owner would get the winnings.

In chariot races, a popular form of entertainment in ancient Rome, a team of four horses pulled each chariot and four to twelve teams competed in each race.

5

On the Water

In addition to the land, water also provided an important method of transportation during ancient times. The simplest and oldest type of boat is the raft. Thousands of years ago, people tied logs or plant stalks together to create these floating vehicles. Another way they made rafts was to cover wooden frames with animal skins. Riders moved the rafts through the water with long poles or paddles.

Another simple watercraft was the canoe. The first canoes were called dugout canoes, because they were made of hollowed-out logs. These boats were large and heavy. Later, people made lighter canoes out of wooden frames covered with bark. The canoes were sealed with tree sap to make them waterproof. Many cultures used canoes, including Native Americans in North America and Polynesians in the Pacific Islands.

Native Americans (above) used short paddles to move their canoes through the water while people in other parts of the world used longer paddles or poles.

Around A.D. 800 the Vikings built fast and powerful longboats that allowed them to travel across the Atlantic Ocean.

By 3000 B.C., Egyptians had replaced paddles with oars. Because oars were fastened to the sides of the boat, they could be pushed harder against the water. This created more power and speed.

Wind power could also be harnessed to move boats. Historians think that the Egyptians made the first sailing ships around 3000 B.C. Their boats had rectangular sails made of papyrus, a paperlike material made from the stems of tall water plants. Later, cloth was used to make the sails.

The Vikings built some of the most powerful boats around A.D. 800. Viking longboats were built of oak. They were long, narrow, and pointed at both ends. This design made the ships fast and easy to move.

Even though they were simple in design, ancient boats could travel long distances. The Vikings traveled across the Atlantic Ocean in their longboats. Scientists also believe that ancient people traveled across the Indian and Pacific oceans in simple rafts and boats.

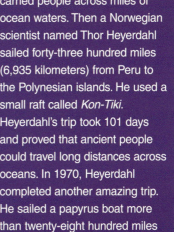

Kon-Tiki

In 1947, few scientists believed that simple boats could have carried people across miles of ocean waters. Then a Norwegian scientist named Thor Heyerdahl sailed forty-three hundred miles (6,935 kilometers) from Peru to the Polynesian islands. He used a small raft called *Kon-Tiki*. Heyerdahl's trip took 101 days and proved that ancient people could travel long distances across oceans. In 1970, Heyerdahl completed another amazing trip. He sailed a papyrus boat more than twenty-eight hundred miles (4,500 kilometers) from North Africa to the island of Barbados in the Caribbean Sea.

Scientist Thor Heyerdahl (far left) builds a papyrus boat in North Africa in 1970.

Exploring the World

Between the 1300s and the 1500s, sailing ships ruled the oceans. Explorers and traders used powerful winds to propel these ships on long voyages. Chinese explorers used westerly winds to travel to India and Africa. European explorers used these winds to travel to North and South America. They used easterly winds to sail back to Europe. Ships traveled these trade routes throughout the year to bring spices, jewels, and other goods from one part of the world to another.

During the 1400s, the caravel was the most popular type of ship. This light, small ship was developed by Spanish and Portuguese explorers. The ship was only about seventy-five feet (twenty-three meters) long. It had long, narrow, triangle-shaped sails called lateens. The shape and position of the lateens allowed them to capture the wind and direct it forward, no matter which direction the wind was coming from. Christopher Columbus used two caravels, the *Niña* and the *Pinta*, when he sailed to America in 1492. Columbus's third ship, the *Santa María*, was a bigger, slower ship called a carrack that was designed to carry cargo.

The Chinese invented a different type of ship for their travels. It was called a junk. A junk's sails were hung on separate panels and controlled by ropes. In bad weather, the sail could be rolled up quickly like a window blind. Junks were also the first ships to use bulkheads, or waterproof

Explorers used charts, maps, compasses and other navigational tools (above) to find their way across the ocean.

This woodcut depicts Christopher Columbus's arrival in the New World. Columbus and other fifteenth-century explorers favored caravels, a type of sailing ship, for their long voyages.

compartments. These made the ship stronger and more seaworthy.

Explorers had several ways to find their way across the ocean. The simplest way to navigate, or find the way, was to follow the stars. Sailors could find where they were on the water by using charts to show the position of the stars. Compasses allowed explorers to steer a straight course when it was too cloudy to see the stars. By the 1400s, detailed maps helped explorers find landmarks and check distances on the map.

FAST FACT

A simple form of the compass was in use as early as the tenth century—more than one thousand years ago.

Carriages and Wagons

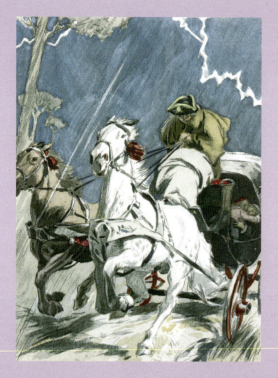

Travel on land changed dramatically during the 1500s. Wealthy and important people began to ride in horse-drawn carriages. These carriages were often very fancy, with elaborate carvings and brightly colored sides. Passengers sat inside, while the driver sat in a seat on the front of the carriage to control the horses.

Over the next hundred years, stagecoaches came into use. These large carriages could carry a number of people. It was not very comfortable to ride in a stagecoach, however. Stagecoaches were often crowded, and the ride was usually bumpy. Rainy weather could turn the roads into mud, which made travel impossible. In dry weather, clouds of dust often flew into the coach. Despite the difficulties, by the

During the 1500s, wealthy people began to ride inside fancy, brightly colored horse-drawn carriages (below). Stagecoaches (above) became a popular form of transportation during the 1700s.

Pioneers used strong and sturdy Conestoga wagons to travel across the country as they moved west.

1700s, stagecoaches were a popular form of transportation in both the United States and Great Britain.

Stagecoaches were useful on well-traveled roads. They could not travel up and down steep hills or over rough land, however. As the American population moved west, it needed a stronger wagon. The Conestoga wagon filled this need.

Conestoga wagons were strong and built to last. Both ends of the wagon curved up so nothing could fall out. A canvas top covered the wagon to protect the inside from rain and the hot sun. Wide, strong wheels helped the wagon travel over rough roads.

The Conestoga was first used in 1717. These sturdy wagons carried farm goods from the Pennsylvania countryside to the city of Philadelphia. By 1800, Conestogas were in use all over the United States. As the pioneers moved west, Conestogas carried their belongings across mountains and deserts.

Conestoga Crossings

Conestoga wagons could even cross streams and rivers. Their wheels were tall and wide, and the body of the wagon was carefully balanced. These features kept the wagon stable even in the water.

Sails and Steam

While travel was changing and improving on land, other changes were taking place on the water. The 1800s brought many improvements in ship design. During the early part of the century, wind power was still the most common way to power a ship. The clipper ship was developed in the early 1800s. These large sailing ships could have more than thirty sails. They traveled more quickly than earlier sailing vessels. In 1818, the first regularly scheduled transatlantic ship service began. Ships crossed the Atlantic Ocean, sailing between New York and London. It could take up to two months to cross the ocean.

The days of the sailing vessels were numbered, however. In 1807, a steam-powered ship called the *Clermont* traveled from New York City to Albany, New York. The 150-mile (241.5-kilometer) trip took just thirty-two hours. The same trip by a wind-powered boat would have taken four days.

In 1819, the first steamship crossed the Atlantic Ocean. Regular service began by 1840. In a steamship, a boiler

Some clipper ships had more than thirty sails, which made them much faster than earlier sailing ships.

heated water to a high temperature until it produced steam. The steam went into a series of cylinders, which caused them to expand and push a piston. The piston turned a flywheel, which then turned a screw that drove an underwater propeller. The propeller moved the ship forward. Steamship service was quicker and more efficient than using wind power. Many people feared that the steam-powered engine in a wooden ship could cause a fire, however.

Until the early 1800s, almost all boats were built of wood, although some iron barges had been constructed in the late 1790s. When wood became scarce in Great Britain, the country had to come up with a new way to build its large fleet of navy and merchant ships. The answer was iron. Iron was stronger and more durable than wood. It was also easier to repair and did not burn.

The first iron steamboat was built in Great Britain in 1821. In 1843, a British company built the first large iron ship that could cross the Atlantic. The combination of iron ships and steam power led to a new age in sea travel. By the late 1800s, the trip from Europe to North America took only fifteen days.

Steamships were made of wood until the early 1800s. Because the steam that powered these vessels was produced by water heated in coal furnaces (opposite), the ships could easily catch fire.

Submarines at War

During the American Revolution, a Connecticut man invented a submarine called the *Turtle*. This submarine was made of wood and was big enough to hold only one person. In 1776, Sergeant Ezra Lee tried to use the *Turtle* against the British navy. He sailed under a British ship called the *Eagle* and tried to fasten a bomb to the *Eagle*. Lee could not attach the bomb, but he and the *Turtle* were able to escape safely.

The Age of Steam

Steam engines made it possible to travel quickly by ship. These engines did not just change water transportation. They also allowed for the development of an entirely new type of land transportation. By the end of the 1800s, steam trains were puffing across most of the world's continents.

A wheeled vehicle can move more easily on a railroad than on a road. The metal rails reduce the friction between the wheels and the road. Friction is caused when two objects rub against each other. This friction slows the objects down and also creates heat. Horse-drawn wagons had used railroads as early as the 1800s. These vehicles used horses to pull wagons along metal tracks. After the invention of the steam locomotive in England in 1804, steam engines replaced horses. These early steam trains carried coal and other goods. England's first passenger train was not built until 1825.

Underground Transportation

Trains did not only travel aboveground. They could also be used underground. The first subway in the world opened in London in 1863.

Steam trains were introduced in the United States in the 1830s and soon became a popular way for Americans to travel.

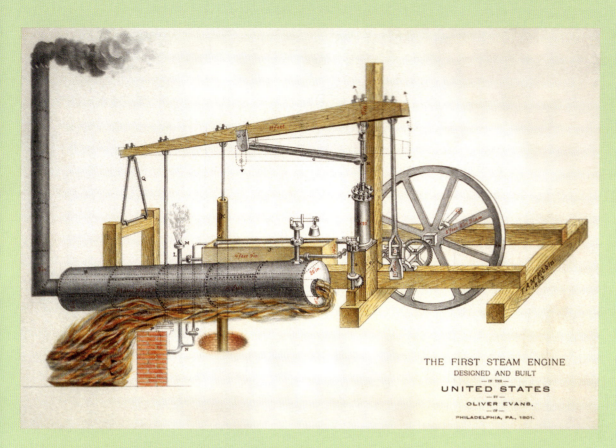

Steam trains work by heating up water in a boiler. The boiler is located in a special engine called a locomotive. Heating the water produces steam. The force of the steam moves a piston, or metal cylinder, back and forth. The piston is connected to the train's wheels. When the piston moves, the wheels turn.

Steam trains came to the United States in 1830, when a train called the Tom Thumb was built. Many people went to see a race between Tom Thumb and a horse, which took place in New York. The horse won, but people were still eager to ride the train.

During the middle of the nineteenth century, steam trains became a popular way to travel in the United States. Then, in 1869, the first transcontinental railroad in the United States was finished. It took six years and more than twenty thousand workers to link the East and West Coasts of the nation with 1,773 miles (2,865 kilometers) of track.

The steam engine allowed faster water transportation by ship and faster land travel by train.

15

The First Automobiles

Some people thought that steam could power cars as well as trains. In 1769, a French engineer named Nicolas-Joseph Cugnot invented a steam-powered gun carriage. This carriage could transport weapons and traveled about three miles per hour. In 1801, a British engineer named Richard Trevithick developed a steam-powered carriage that could travel up to nine miles an hour.

Steam engines were large and heavy. This was not a problem when they were used in large vehicles, such as trains. The steam engine was too big, however, to use in a small vehicle like a car. A different kind of engine was needed.

During the 1860s and 1870s, internal combustion engines were developed. These engines burned fuel inside the engine. In 1883, a German engineer named Gottlieb Daimler built the first successful gasoline engine. Two years later, another German, Carl Benz, built the first

Nicolas-Joseph Cugnot invented a steam-powered carriage that traveled three miles per hour (top). Carl Benz (pictured) improved on the steam engine and built the first gasoline-powered car.

gasoline-powered car. This early car had only three wheels.

The first cars looked like horse-drawn carriages, only without the horse. Each car was made by hand, which made them very expensive. During the first few years of the 1900s, cars seemed like a dangerous toy that only a few very rich people would own. Many people thought that horse-drawn carriages would continue to provide transportation. Then new technology changed the way cars were made.

Some cars in the late 1800s and early 1900s had electric engines because they were quiet and did not scare horses or pedestrians.

Electric Cars

Today there is a lot of talk about electric cars, but these cars are not a new idea. During the late 1800s and early 1900s, electric engines were used in several different car models. People liked them because they were quiet and less likely to scare horses or pedestrians. Most electric cars could travel about thirty miles (forty-eight kilometers) per hour. They could only travel about fifty miles (eighty kilometers), however, before the batteries needed to be recharged. By 1930, gasoline engines had become a more popular way to power a car. Electric cars were no longer manufactured on a large scale.

Automobiles and Motorcycles Take over the Roads

During the early 1900s, cars were expensive and hard to make. That all changed in 1903 when a man named Henry Ford started the Ford Motor Company. Five years later, Ford began to make a car called the Model T. This car was small and cheap enough that most families could afford one. What set the Model T apart from earlier cars was the way it was built. This car was built on an assembly line. Machines moved the parts to people at workstations around the factory. Each person had a specific job, such as installing the headlights. This type of production allowed the cars to be built quickly and cheaply. The Model T was a great success. More than 15 million of these cars were sold between

Henry Ford (left) manufactured the Model T using an assembly line (below), a fast and cheap way to build cars.

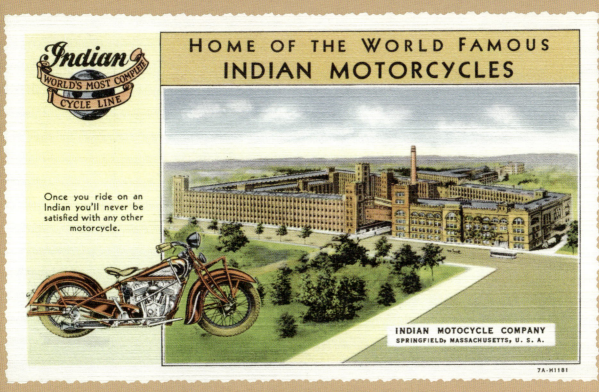

The Indian Motorcycle Company began making motorcycles designed especially for police officers in the 1920s.

1908 and 1927. In 1925, a Model T cost about $260, which would be about $2,600 today.

Motorcycles also became more popular during the early part of the twentieth century. The first motorcycles were just bicycles with an engine attached. Steam engines were used at first, but were soon replaced with gasoline engines. In 1885, Gottlieb Daimler attached two wheels to a wooden frame. Then he added a horse's saddle to make a seat. His son Paul was the first rider of this odd-looking motorcycle.

Motorcycles became popular with police officers. They were faster than cars and could maneuver easily in tight spaces. By the 1920s, an American company called Indian Motorcycle Company was making motorcycles that were specially designed for police officers.

During wartime, soldiers found the motorcycle was a handy way to get around. Like policemen, soldiers needed to move quickly and travel on rough roads where cars could not go. Scouts often used motorcycles to carry messages from one army unit to another.

The Development of the Bicycle

In 1855, many French people liked to ride a type of bicycle called a velocipede. The velocipede had a wooden frame and iron tires. The front tire was much larger than the rear tire. Pedals were used to propel the bike. In England, this was called the bone shaker, because it created such a bumpy ride.

The safety bicycle was developed around 1880. This bicycle had two rubber tires of the same size. The safety bicycle became very popular in the United States. About 1 million bicycles a year were produced in the United States between 1899 and 1909.

Trucks transported goods and soldiers during World War I.

Trucks and Highways

Cars and motorcycles were not the only gas-powered vehicles on the road during the 1900s. Trucks became popular during this era as well. One of the first trucks was a gas-powered wagon built by Gottlieb Daimler in 1896. This wagon had an open compartment for the driver in the front and carried freight in the enclosed back section.

The mass production of trucks began just before World War I started in 1914. During the war, trucks were often used as ambulances to transport injured soldiers from the battlefield to the hospital.

In the early days, trucks were mostly used for local deliveries because there were not enough good roads

Buses

Cars and trucks have shared the highways with buses since the early 1900s. The first buses were pulled by horses. By 1905, however, New York City began the first motorized bus service. By 1930, thousands of bus services operated in cities around the country. Today, buses are the most-used form of mass transportation in the United States.

between cities. As roads improved, these large, heavy vehicles soon became an important way to move goods around the country.

In 1916, the U.S. government passed the Federal Aid Road Act. This act promoted the building of paved roads between cities. Before then, most roads were dirt paths that had originally been used as horse trails. While horses could travel over bumpy, muddy roads, motorized vehicles could not. The Federal Aid Road Act made it easier for vehicles to travel between cities. This improved travel and business throughout the country.

As the nation's highway system expanded and improved, so did the use of trucks to move goods from place to place. By 1918, there were more than six hundred thousand trucks on the road in the United States.

High Speed Driving

During the 1930s, the Germans built the world's first superhighway. This highway was called the autobahn. The autobahn was the first road specially designed to allow drivers to travel at high speeds over long distances.

Adolf Hitler (right) initiated the building of Germany's autobahn.

Taking to the Air

There had been many changes in land and water transportation by the early 1900s. Some people, however, wanted to travel in a whole new way. They wanted to take to the air.

On December 17, 1903, Orville Wright piloted the *Flyer* into the air for a twelve-second, 120-foot (36.5-meter) flight in Kitty Hawk, North Carolina. Wright had built the plane with his brother Wilbur. Their craft was a biplane, which means it had two sets of wings. The width of the plane's wings, or wingspan, measured just over forty feet (twelve meters).

Airplanes can fly because air moves over and under the wings at different speeds. The air pressure under the wing is higher. This causes the air to push up against the wings and lift the plane into the air.

In 1903, Orville Wright (left) piloted the Flyer, *which he built with his brother Wilbur (above left), for a twelve-second flight at Kitty Hawk, North Carolina (below).*

The airship Hindenburg *exploded in a huge fire fed by hydrogen gas as it attempted to land at Lakehurst, New Jersey, in 1937.*

During World War I, planes were used to spy on enemy positions and fire on enemy aircraft. Some also dropped bombs. After the war, many pilots performed in air shows around the world. These pilots were called barnstormers, and they thrilled audiences with their daring tricks.

At the same time airplanes were being developed, other inventors worked to develop the helicopter. In 1907, a Frenchman named Paul Cornu became the first person to rise vertically in powered flight. His helicopter used two rotors, or blades, attached to a metal frame. This machine was hard to control, though. It was not until 1936 that a German inventor created the FA-61. The FA-61 was the first practical design for a helicopter. Several were manufactured and used during World War II.

Up, Up, and Away

Airships were huge bags filled with hydrogen, a gas that is lighter than air and allowed the ship to fly. Passengers and crew rode in a cabin underneath the hydrogen bag.

The Germans called airships zeppelins. Zeppelins carried passengers between Germany and the United States for several years during the 1930s. Then, on May 6, 1937, a zeppelin called the *Hindenburg* caught fire while landing at Lakehurst, New Jersey. Thirty-six people were killed in the spectacular fire fed by the hydrogen gas. Few people wanted to travel by zeppelin after the disaster.

23

Changing Trains

Today's high-speed computer trains allow people to live in the suburbs and work in the city.

While new technology was creating ways to travel through the air, changes in transportation were occurring on the ground as well. During the middle of the twentieth century, railroads became an important type of transportation throughout the world. By the late 1930s, steam engines had been replaced by engines that ran on diesel fuel or electric power. These trains were cheaper to run and could travel longer distances at higher speeds. Diesel and electric engines needed less maintenance than steam engines. They were also cleaner. Today, most trains use a combination of diesel and electric power.

Trains became an efficient way to travel long distances between major cities. On May 26, 1934, a train called the Zephyr traveled from Denver, Colorado, to Chicago, Illinois, without stopping. This was a distance of more than one thousand miles. The Zephyr also set a speed record, traveling at more than 112 miles (180 kilometers) per hour. Cities in Europe, Japan, and other countries are also linked by trains.

Trains are also used within cities. Commuter railroads bring workers into cities from surrounding suburbs.

Trains do not just move people. They also move freight. Specially designed train cars can carry just about anything. Tank cars carry liquids such as oil or ink.

Refrigerated cars carry coal or gravel. Other goods are carried in large metal boxes called containers. These containers can be moved easily from ship to train to truck.

Many freight trains had a small car called a caboose at the very end of the train. The caboose provided shelter for the train crew. It was a good place for the conductor to watch the entire train as it moved along the tracks. Cabooses are no longer in use, although they can sometimes be seen on older trains.

In 1934, the Zephyr set a speed record as it traveled nonstop from Denver to Chicago at more than 112 miles per hour.

Flying Fast

> **FAST FACT**
> Between 1976 and 2000, the Concorde was the only airplane to provide regular supersonic service between Europe and the United States. It flew at twice the speed of sound and could cross the Atlantic Ocean in less than four hours.

Trains could carry people fairly quickly over long distances. The airplane was another way to go on long trips. There were still problems to work out before airplanes could become a practical method of transportation, however.

Although commercial airplane service had been around since 1914, the early days of flying were not very comfortable for the passengers. During the 1920s, planes had no heat or air conditioning. Flights were so bumpy that most passengers became very ill. The first flight attendants were nurses hired to care for sick passengers.

Until the 1940s, most airplanes were powered by an internal combustion engine. The engine turned

In 1947, Chuck Yeager became the first person to fly faster than the speed of sound.

The Concorde was a supersonic airplane that could cross the Atlantic Ocean in less than four hours.

one or more propellers on the front of the plane. Propeller-driven planes could not fly very fast or very far. A more powerful engine was needed.

The first jet engines were designed during the 1930s. Jet engines work by sending a stream of hot gas backward. The force of the gas pushes the plane forward.

During World War II (1939–1945), the military in the United States, Great Britain, Germany, and Japan developed many different kinds of jet fighters. After the war ended, these advances were used to improve commercial aircraft. In 1952, the first commercial jet began regular flights between Great Britain and South Africa.

Early jets could fly about 550 miles (885.5 kilometers) an hour. That was fast, but pilots kept pushing the limit of speed. On October 14, 1947, Chuck Yeager became the first person to fly faster than the speed of sound (660 miles or 966 kilometers per hour). Until Yeager accomplished this feat, some scientists thought it was impossible. Yeager's flight proved these scientists wrong. It also opened the door for an entirely new kind of travel—space travel.

Space Travel

To travel into space, vehicles had to travel fast enough to escape Earth's gravity. Gravity is the force that pulls things down toward the surface of Earth. During the twentieth century, scientists developed rockets that could propel vehicles into space. Rockets are the only engines that can operate in space, where there is no oxygen. They carry fuel and their own oxygen supply.

In 1957, the Soviet Union launched the first space satellite, *Sputnik*. By the 1960s, both the Soviet Union and the United States had launched rockets that carried dogs and monkeys into space. These flights showed that living things could survive a spaceflight.

On April 12, 1961, Soviet Yuri Gagarin became the first man in space. On May 5, the first American traveled into space when Alan Shepard took a fifteen-minute flight.

Before they could send humans into space, both the Soviet Union and the United States launched rockets that carried dogs and monkeys to prove that living things could survive space flight.

Seconds after liftoff, the space shuttle Challenger *exploded, killing all seven astronauts onboard.*

The U.S. space program developed quickly during the 1960s. On July 16, 1969, a ship called *Apollo 11* lifted off from Cape Canaveral Space Center in Florida. Four days later, a small craft called the lunar module separated from the ship and landed on the moon. For the first time, humans walked on another world.

On April 12, 1981, the first space shuttle lifted into space. The space shuttle was powered by a huge rocket that separated from the craft and returned to Earth. The shuttle itself then orbited Earth and returned to land on a runway like an airplane.

Tragedies in Space

On January 28, 1986, the shuttle *Challenger* exploded after liftoff, killing the seven astronauts onboard. The disaster was caused when rubber rings cracked and flames escaped from the rocket and ignited the fuel.

In January 2003, the shuttle *Columbia* blasted off into space. During liftoff, a piece of foam broke off and hit one of the shuttle's wings. On February 1, the *Columbia* disintegrated as it reentered Earth's atmosphere. Investigators believe that when the foam hit the wing, it damaged some heat-resistant tiles. This caused the wing and the left side of the shuttle to become too hot.

Prehistory

500 B.C.

100 B.C.

A.D. 100

200

500

1000

1200

1300

1400

1500

1600

1700

1800

1900

2000

2100

France's TGV train travels at speeds of up to 186 miles per hour.

Transportation Today

People have always looked for faster and cleaner ways to travel. Train travel has changed from smoky, slow steam engines to faster, quieter electric trains. Today's fastest trains are found in Europe. France's TGV travels at an average speed of 186 miles (299 kilometers) per hour. This electric train has a special streamlined shape to help it travel quickly.

Even faster trains are in development. Maglev trains use a combination of giant magnets and electricity to travel quickly and quietly. These trains use only a single rail and can travel at about 200 miles (322 kilometers) an hour.

Cars are also being changed and improved. American car companies began to produce electric cars in the 1990s, but these cars could not travel long distances without stopping to recharge the battery. Today, several companies sell hybrid cars. These cars use a combination of a gas-powered engine and an electric battery. They are

Jet-Powered People?

Scientists have created rocket-powered jet packs that allow a person to fly. They are made of tanks loaded with fuel. When the fuel is lit, powerful steam flows from nozzles connected to the tanks and provides power. They are very heavy, hard to control, and cannot fly very far.

quieter, cleaner, and use less gasoline than regular cars. In the future, cars may be powered by fuel cells that use chemical reactions between hydrogen and oxygen to create electricity.

Some scientists are working to prevent accidents by creating sophisticated computers inside cars. These computers will be able to sense when other cars, pedestrians, or objects are too close to the car. The computer will then stop or slow the car automatically.

It may become easier to travel without a car in the future. In 2002, an inventor named Dean Kamen introduced the Segway Human Transporter. This two-wheeled scooter moves in response to the rider's body. If the rider leans forward, the Segway moves forward. A system of sensors keeps the Segway and its rider balanced. An electric motor in each wheel moves the vehicle.

Thousands of years ago, people had only their own two feet and the power of animals to help them move. They could never have dreamed of today's cars, airplanes, spaceships, and high-speed trains. The future is certain to hold just as many more unimaginable surprises.

Modern modes of transportation, such as the Segway Human Transporter, point to the future of travel.

Glossary

bulkhead: A waterproof compartment inside a ship.
diesel: A type of fuel.
freight: Goods or cargo carried by train, ship, truck, or plane.
friction: When two objects rub against each other.
hybrid: Something that is made of two different things.
locomotive: An engine used to push or pull railroad cars.
navigate: To use maps or other tools as a guide.
papyrus: A paperlike material made from the stems of a tall water plant.
streamlined: Designed to move quickly through air or water.
transcontinental: Across a continent.

For More Information

Books
Antonio Casanellas, *Great Discoveries and Inventions That Improved Transportation*. Milwaukee, WI: Gareth Stevens, 1999.
Tim McNeese, *Conestogas and Stagecoaches*. New York: Crestwood House, 1993.
Judith E. Rinard, *The Smithsonian Air and Space Museum Book of Flight*. Buffalo, NY: Firefly, 2001.
Richard Steins, *Transportation Milestones and Breakthroughs*. Austin, TX: Raintree Steck-Vaughn, 1995.
Michael Woods and Mary B. Woods, *Ancient Transportation: From Camels to Canals*. Minneapolis: Runestone, 2000.

Web Sites
Air Transportation (www.nasm.si.edu). This site from the National Air and Space Museum displays photos of historic airplanes and flying machines.
How Stuff Works: Transportation (www.howstuffworks.com). This Web site includes a number of articles describing how automobiles and engines operate.
National Railroad Historical Society (www.nrhs.com). This Web site includes historical photos of trains from the past.
Transportation Timeline (http://inventors.about.com/library/inventors/bl_history_of_transportation.htm). This time line includes many important dates in the history of transportation.

Index

airplanes, 22–23, 26
ambulance, 20
animals, 4
assembly line, 18
automobiles, 16–19

Benz, Carl, 17
bicycle, 19
boats, 6–9, 12–13
buses, 20

carriages, 10–11
cars, 16–19, 30
carts, 5
chariots, 5
Conestoga wagon, 10, 11

Daimler, Gottlieb, 17, 19, 20

electric cars, 17, 30
explorers, 8–9

flying, 26–27
Ford, Henry, 18
fuel, 24

gasoline engine, 17

helicopter, 23

internal combustion engine, 16–17, 26
iron, 12–13

jet packs, 30
jets, 26–27

mass production, 20
mass transportation, 20
Model T, 18
motorcycles, 18–19

railroads, 14–15, 24–25
roads, 20–21
rockets, 28–29
sailing ships, 7, 8, 12

Segway Human Transporter, 30–31
space travel, 28–29
stagecoach, 10
steam, 12, 14–15, 19, 24
steamship, 12–13
submarines, 13
subway, 14
supersonic travel, 27

trains, 14–15, 24–25, 30
trucks, 20–21

wagons, 10–11
water transportation, 6–9, 12–13
wheel, 4–5
wind, 6–7, 8, 12
Wright brothers, 22

Yeager, Chuck, 27

zeppelin, 23